For Emilio!
We'll be friends
forever!
Merry Christmas!
-1982

Love, Susan

DUNOYER DE SEGONZAC

A. Dunoyer de Segonzac

by ANNE DISTEL

CROWN PUBLISHERS, INC. - NEW YORK

Title page: SELF-PORTRAIT, 1925
Ink drawing and wash, 8⅝" × 6⅝" (22 × 17.5 cm)
Private collection, Paris

Translated from the French by:
ALICE SACHS

Collection published under the direction of:
MADELEINE LEDIVELEC-GLOECKNER

PHOTOGRAPHS

Bibliothèque Nationale, Paris – Thierry Chatel, Viroflay – Giraudon, Paris – E. B. Heston, Columbus, Ohio – J. Hyde, Paris – Bruce C. Jones, Huntington, New York – R. Lalance, Meudon-la-Forêt – Gene Lester, Los Angeles – Otto E. Nelson, New York – Eric Pollitzer, New York – Maurice Poplin, Villemomble, Seine-St. Denis – Service de Documentation Photographique du Musée National d'Art Moderne, Paris – Service de Documentation Photographique de la Réunion des Musées Nationaux, Paris – John Webb, London.

Library of Congress Cataloging in Publication Data
Dayez-Distel, Anne.
    Dunoyer de Segonzac.

    Bibliography: p. 95
    Includes index.
    1. Segonzac, André Dunoyer de, 1884–1974.
I. Title.
N6853.S4D39   760'.092'4   79–19720
ISBN 0–517–54004–5

LIBRARY OF CONGRESS CATALOG CARD NUMBER: ISBN: 0–517–54004–5
PRINTED IN ITALY – © 1980 BONFINI PRESS CORPORATION, NAEFELS, SWITZERLAND
ALL RIGHTS TO THE ILLUSTRATIONS RESERVED BY S.P.A.D.E.M., PARIS
ALL RIGHTS IN THE U.S.A. ARE RESERVED BY CROWN PUBLISHERS, INC., NEW YORK, NEW YORK

THE BAR AT THE PALACE, 1906. Watercolor on paper, 7½″ × 9¹³/₁₆″ (19 × 25 cm)
Private collection, Paris

The name of André Dunoyer de Segonzac is one of the best-known names in the gallery of French twentieth-century painters. He immediately made an impression with the first works he exhibited in 1910, was well known by 1914, and famous by the 1920–1925 period; at no time after that, during a long and uninterrupted career, until his death in 1974, did his popularity wane in France. His art evolved in the course of these sixty-five years, but the artist always remained loyal to his original concept of what art should be. This consistency is underlined by the continuity of the themes treated by the painter: landscapes of the Ile-de-France and the South of France, still lifes depicting the same familiar objects, and figures in landscapes. Few major events, or at least events that seemed to affect him, left their mark on Segonzac's art; his life was apparently serene, except possibly for the cruel experience of the First World War. Yet, we are constantly aware of

5

STUDY FOR THE «ROWERS», undated. Oil on canvas, 24″ × 36¼″ (61 × 92 cm)
Musées Nationaux, France. Gift of Pierre Lévy

THE ROWERS (STUDY), undated. Watercolor, $18^{1}/_{16}'' \times 24''$ (46 × 61 cm)
Private collection

the echoes of staunch friendships for other artists, writers, and poets, which frequently vibrate in the artist's works with recognizable impact. Segonzac's art is multifaceted. Whether he used oils or watercolors, he showed himself to be a painter above all. The powerful originality of this master artist is further underlined by his contributions in the fields of drawing and engraving, including his work as a book illustrator.

From the beginning of his career, Dunoyer de Segonzac never failed to attract the attention of critics in his country. Numerous studies and articles, pertaining to every aspect of his activities, were devoted to him. For the most part, the authors of these reviews were friends of the artist or collectors of his work; in addition, he himself analyzed in detail and defended his aesthetic efforts on many different occasions. All this warm, lively, perceptive testimony helps us understand and realize fully the importance of the art of Dunoyer de Segonzac, one of the important figures in the art of the twentieth century.

THE BEGINNINGS

André Dunoyer de Segonzac was born on July 7, 1884, in Boussy-Saint-Antoine (Val-de-Marne), on property owned by his grandparents. His father, Louis, descended from an ancient family of southwestern France, was a naval officer; his mother, Marie-Amélie, was the granddaughter of Jean-Charles Persin, a cabinet minister under Louis-Philippe, who was made famous by Daumier's caricatures of him. Segonzac had all the benefits of a good social background. His childhood was spent in part in the country, in Boussy, and in part in Paris, where his parents resided on Boulevard Saint-Germain. He attended Louis-le-Grand and Henri IV schools and graduated in 1900. Although in his family, with the exception of his mother, no one had shown any artistic leanings, Segonzac's interest in drawing and painting manifested itself early, while he was still an adolescent. Giving up their ambition to see him enter the military academy of Saint-Cyr, his parents authorized him to enroll at the Free Academy of Luc-Olivier Merson, which perpetuated a type of academic instruction inherited from the nineteenth century that Segonzac immediately rejected. His military service temporarily interrupted his artistic studies, but afforded him the opportunity to meet Jean-Louis Boussingault, who also wished to become a painter; their friendship was an enduring one. For some time Segonzac worked in the studio of Jean-Paul Laurens, another traditionalist of the school who specialized in historical paintings, then at the Académie de la Palette, whose staff members included Desvallières, Guérin, Dethomas and Jacques-Emile Blanche. It was there that he made the acquaintance of Albert Mainssieux and Luc-Albert Moreau, who would remain his friends. Segonzac himself considered 1906 the date of his « debut. » It can be stated with certainty that his decision to work alone, independent of any specific teacher, symbolized by his move shortly afterward to a studio that he shared with Boussingault, at 37 rue Saint-André-des-Arts, marked the true beginning of his professional career.

Segonzac was a member of that fortunate generation that initiated the spectacular changes that transformed painting between 1900 and 1914. He was younger than Matisse, but a contemporary of Picasso, Braque, and of all the Cubists. Like them, Segonzac frequented museums. He particularly admired Rembrandt, Delacroix, and Courbet (he later acquired Courbet's *The Trout*, which was installed in the Louvre in 1978.) In the Luxembourg Museum, he saw the Impressionist paintings in the Caillebotte Collection, which were already being widely imitated. At that time, Renoir, and especially Monet, (who died in 1919 and 1926 respectively), although their reputations were finally established, had not yet produced the full measure of their artistic achievements.

THE DRINKERS (A CABARET), 1910. Oil on canvas, 63$^{13}/_{16}''$ × 51$^{1}/_{8}''$ (162 × 130)
Musée National d'Art Moderne
Centre National d'Art et de Culture Georges Pompidou, Paris

VENUS DE MEDICI, 1908. Oil on canvas, 36¼″ × 28¾″ (92 × 73 cm)
Musée National d'Art Moderne. Centre National d'Art et de Culture Georges Pompidou, Paris

STILL LIFE (VENUS DE MEDICI), 1912. Oil on canvas, 36¼″ × 28¾″ (92 × 73 cm)
Musée National d'Art Moderne. Centre National d'Art et de Culture Georges Pompidou, Paris

THE VILLAGE, 1910. Oil on canvas, 36¼″ × 28¾″ (92 × 73 cm). Private collection, Paris

THE PICNIC (FANCY BREADLOAVES), c. 1912–1913. Oil on canvas, 28¾″ × 36¼″ (73 × 92 cm)
Musée National d'Art Moderne
Centre National d'Art et de Culture Georges Pompidou, Paris

Two Nudes, 1911. Oil on canvas, $25^{5}/_{8}'' \times 78^{3}/_{4}''$ (65 × 200 cm)
Musée National d'Art Moderne. Centre National d'Art et de Culture Georges Pompidou, Paris

14

LYING NUDE WITH BLUE SCARF, 1911. Oil on panel, $14^9/_{16}'' \times 21^3/_4''$ (37 × 55 cm)
Musée National d'Art Moderne. Centre National d'Art et de Culture Georges Pompidou, Paris

Landscape and Small Road at Périgny, c. 1912–1913
Oil on canvas, 23⅝″ × 36¼″ (60 × 92 cm). Musée Nationaux, France. Gift of Pierre Lévy

16

The River from Yerres at Périgny, c. 1912.   Pen on paper, 11$^{13}/_{16}$″ × 18$^{5}/_{16}$″ (30 × 46.5 cm)
Musée du Louvre, Cabinet des Dessins, Paris

Three Dancers (Russian Dancers), 1910
Pen and ink drawing on paper, $6^5/_{16}'' \times 8^1/_2''$ (16×21.6 cm)
Private collection, Paris

18

Nijinsky, 1911. Pen and ink drawing on paper, 8¹¹/₁₆″ × 5¹/₈″ (22 × 13.8 cm)
Private collection, Paris

Isadora Duncan, 1910. Pen an ink drawing, 10¼" × 8¼" (26 × 21 cm)
Private collection, Paris

MID-LENT, 1911. Oil on paper, $18\,^7/_8{}'' \times 24\,^{13}/_{16}{}''$ (48 × 63 cm)
Musée National d'Art Moderne. Centre National d'Art et de Culture Georges Pompidou, Paris

The Pugilists   **LES BOXEURS**   Die Faustkämpfer

1911

Appartient à l'artiste

Boxing Match, 1911. Reproduction of a painting destroyed

Like all the young artists of his generation, and also of the preceding generation, who were trying to blaze new trails, he studied the work of Cézanne, who had just died. One name inscribed by Segonzac's pen on a number of occasions was that of Douanier Rousseau, whose natural boldness and profound poetic sense also appealed to Delaunay, Apollinaire, Braque and Picasso. Was he responsive to the colors employed by Van Gogh or those used by the Fauves, who caused a sensation in the press on the occasion of the Salon d'Automne of 1905? It would appear not, even though some of the rare works of this period that have come down to us testify to the fact that bright, intense coloring held a strong appeal for him. Unlike Matisse, Delaunay, Braque, and Metzinger, the Pointillist technique of the Neo-Impressionists does not seem to have interested him, although he encountered Signac during a first visit to Saint-Tropez in 1908. Nor, according to what evidence we have, was he especially attracted by the art of Bonnard or Vuillard.

THE PREWAR PERIOD (1908–1914)

In 1908 Dunoyer de Segonzac exhibited for the first time in the Salon d'Automne, a liberal institution that was open to young artists. Until 1922 he regularly submitted pictures to this Salon, showing nothing thereafter until 1937 and, after that, exhibiting only at irregular intervals. His submissions of 619, *Study of a Nude*, and 620, *Tartanes*, both directly inspired by the visit he had just made to Saint-Tropez, seem to have been overlooked by the critics. The same is not true of the paintings exhibited in the spring of 1909 at the Salon des Indépendants (535, *Still Life*, and 536, *Study of a Nude*). Roger-Marx wrote in «Chronique des Arts,» apropos of the private preview of this Salon's show: «Room 17: Van Dongen, Metzinger, Verhoeven, Marinot. Their artistic goals are such that they are better adapted to creating decorative art than they are to producing easel painting. The same can certainly not be said for Messrs. Le Fauconnier, Boussingault, and Dunoyer de Segonzac. However unexpected the exteriors in which they envelop their fundamental powers, the existence of their talent cannot be gainsaid; one can only hope that they will find opportunities to develop it more normally and to act more judiciously and appropriately to achieve their goals.» This criticism is slightly Sibylline, especially in view of the fact that we do not definitely know what works Segonzac showed. In any case, the gifts and the originality of the neophyte were being acknowledged by one of the most widely read and respected critics of the period. Gradually, the name of Segonzac also became associated with the spare, incisive drawings that were appearing in contemporary periodicals. His contributions to a number of illustrated publications would continue until the war. Among these, we can cite the «Grande Revue» of Rouché, the «Bulletin de l'Œuvre» of Lugné-Poë (affiliated with the theatre about which we shall have the occasion to speak again), «Panurge,» «La Vie,» «Le Témoin,» «Montjoie,» and later, during the war, «L'Elan» and «Le Crapouillot.»

Yet this activity as an illustrator never outweighed his parallel career as a painter. In 1910 Segonzac again exhibited at the Indépendants (1618, *Decorative Panel* and 1619, *Nude*). The response of the critics to these submissions was negative. André Salmon («Paris-Journal,» March 18, 1910), declared: «A Fauve whom it is impossible to classify, not really a Cubist, a man whose work was justifiably hung in an unfavorable place, Denoyer [*sic*] de Segonzac piles up untidy nudes; the ensemble has the effect of hideous rose-colored masonry.» Apollinaire echoed him in «L'Intransigeant» of March 22, 1910: «We really do not know what to say about Mr. Dunoyer de Segonzac. He wastes a great deal of canvas and color to no useful end.» Let us immediately add that these two critics rapidly changed their opinions. Once more Segonzac did not fail to be noticed.

SCAFFOLD POLES, 1920. Pen and watercolor on paper, $24\,^5/_{16}''\times18\,^1/_{16}''$ (61.7 × 46 cm)
Musée National d'Art Moderne. Centre National d'Art et de Culture Georges Pompidou, Paris

If the works previously mentioned, that were exhibited in the Salons, are difficult to identify, the painting featured in Salon d'Automne of 1910 (in which were prominently displayed the panels of *Dance* and *Music*, painted by Matisse for the town house of Shchukin in Moscow, panels now in the Hermitage), has always remained in the foreground of the painter's works. We are referring to *A Cabaret*, better known under the title *The Drinkers.* * Everyone is in agreement that this represents a decisive step forward in the artist's career. Over and beyond the recognizable influences of the art of Courbet, Daumier, and Cézanne, that the critics took pleasure in pointing out, there is present the mark of a very original temperament. It is true that the subject itself to some extent recalls the Cézanne of the *Card Players*, but the spirit and the realism of the picture are a far cry from Cézanne's painting. The very special technique of superimposing layers of thick paint on one another, smoothed out by a palette knife (the canvas had to be pasted onto a panel, the better to support the weight of the materials), is rather reminiscent of the works of Cézanne's youth, such as the *Portrait of the Artist's Father* (Washington, D.C., National Gallery). In any case, this work appears to represent a studied reaction against the light painting that was bungled by the clumsy and untalented imitators of the Impressionists. Segonzac was not the only painter to set his feet along this path; nevertheless, *The Drinkers* occupies a unique place in the artistic annals of the period. The famous couturier Paul Poiret, then at the height of his renown, acquired this painting. This was the first of many of Segonzac's works acquired by Poiret, all of which were scattered when Poiret's possessions were sold in 1925. Moreover, Segonzac valued this painting very highly and bought it back in order to donate it to the Musée d'Art Moderne in Paris in 1963. The meeting between Poiret and Segonzac, presumably through the good offices of Boussingault, did not result in merely one single purchase. Segonzac's participation in the organization of the galas given by the couturier in his home on the Faubourg Saint-Honoré, together with that of Dufy and Vlaminck, was one of the notable events in the artist's career and the history of Parisian taste in the prewar period. Thus it was that Segonzac, along with Dufy, Fauconnet and Naudin, created the decor and costumes for the Persian fete, « The Thousand and Second Night, » given in June 1911, and « Fête of the Kings, » or « Fêtes of Bacchus, » in 1912, at the Pavillon du Butard. Photographs show Segonzac, superb in a splendid costume and turban, on the occasion of these entertainments. Other documents evoke the sojourns of the artist on the island of Tudy, where Poiret owned property, and a cruise on the Mediterranean on one of the couturier's boats. It may seem paradoxical that the magnificent Poiret should be attracted by the austere paintings of Segonzac, but this undoubtedly says something about the taste of the collector of the works of Dufy, Vlaminck, Derain, La Fresnaye, Boussingault, Matisse, Marie Laurencin, Van Dongen, Picasso, and so on.

It was through the intervention of Paul Poiret, who had been selected by Jacques Rouché of the Théâtre des Arts to design the costumes for the « Nebuchadnezzar » of Maurice de Faramond, that Segonzac made his debut in the field of theatrical décor. The maquettes of the décors executed for this production were shown at the Salon d'Automne of 1911, and Marc Elder commented: « The deep purple of Nebuchadnezzar's costume is seen in the midst of green and orange materials that shimmer and move with the swaying of the dancers, and live bodies quiver tremulously along the lengths of their spines. » (« La Vie, » August 31, 1912).

It was also in 1910 that two albums of Segonzac's drawings were issued, both of them focusing on the dance. The one entitled *Scheherazade, 24 Drawings of a Russian Ballet*, were inspired by Diaghilev's company, to whose performances Parisians were flocking. The enthusiasm aroused by the Ballets Russes, that could be seen at the Châtelet in 1909, was immense. Technical

---

* See p. 9.

*The Plain of Brie (in France), c. 1913. Pen and India ink, 9¹/₁₆″ × 13³/₄″ (23 × 35 cm)
Private collection, Paris*

The Attack, 1914–1918. Pen, India ink and wash on paper, 6¹¹/₁₆″ × 12³/₁₆″ (17 × 31 cm)
Musée des Deux Guerres Mondiales, Paris

perfection, inspiration, beauty, and originality touched with exoticism were miraculously combined; legendary dancers — Fokine, Nijinsky, Anna Pavlova, Ida Rubinstein, Karsavina, Bolm, Monakov, and others — pirouetted on Bakst's brilliant sets. It was in 1910, at the time when the company had found a house in the Paris Opera, and «Scheherazade,» conceived by Bakst and Fokine with music by Rimsky-Korsakov, was created, that Segonzac did the first of his drawings inspired by the Ballets Russes.* These drawings in India ink were executed from life during the rehearsals and finished performances that the artist frequently attended. After «Scheherazade,» Stravinsky's «Firebird» provided Segonzac with a subject for new studies. Other sketches evoke, by a single rapid stroke, sometimes underlined by a few black highlights, Fokine in «The Carnival» of Schumann, or Nijinsky leaping in «The Specter of the Rose» in 1911.** Segonzac can be numbered among the first French artists to show an interest in the Ballets Russes. As he himself made clear, Picasso, Matisse, and Derain came to the ballet only later, introduced to it by Cocteau; still, unlike Segonzac, these painters collaborated directly in some of the ballets of the postwar period.

In the same year that marked the appearance of the *Scheherazade* album, there was issued another collection of drawings devoted to Isadora Duncan,*** preceded by an explanatory foreword by Fernand Divoire, that was well received by Apollinaire («La Vie Artistique,» May 10, 1911), even though the latter did not appreciate the experimental choreography of the famous dancer. As in the case of the Ballets Russes, the drawings, done by pen in India ink and inspired by Isadora Duncan, were done on the spot, in the auditorium of the Gaieté Lyrique, where the dancer had been appearing since 1909. Segonzac was deeply moved by Isadora's personality. His drawings, admirable in their spontaneity and evocation of rhythmic movements (some of them were shown in the Salon d'Automne of 1911), did not give birth to any paintings, any more than had the drawings of the Ballets Russes. It is evident that what Segonzac wished to express in these silhouetted figures with indistinct faces, caught in arrested attitudes of a moment's duration, was the mobility of the human body. It is interesting to compare these drawings to those that Rodin did of Isadora. Two of them, reproduced in the «Bulletin de Œuvre» of Lugné-Poë devoted to Isadora Duncan (November 1911), clearly show that Rodin was more impressed by the «Hellenism» of the dancer. But this same bulletin, in addition to featuring Rodin, pays homage to the young Dunoyer de Segonzac, whose name in this connection does not appear inappropriate, even alongside that of the brilliant sculptor.

Segonzac's submission to the Indépendants of 1911 (No. 2020, *Group of Nudes*, and 2021, *Landscape*) once more attracted attention. André Salmon commented: «The nudes are elegantly constructed, tidy but powerful . . .» («Paris-Journal,» April 20, 1911), while Apollinaire observed: «Dunoyer de Segonzac, who knows how, in his drawings, to pin down the grace of choreographic movements, summons up his will-power to paint powerfully. His group of nudes, accurately observed, proves to us that his palette possesses humanity. He is also exhibiting a delicate *Landscape*.» («L'Intransigeant,» April 21, 1911). The *Group of Nudes* is not clearly identifiable (even though we may assume that this may refer to the large canvas, dated 1911, and recently displayed in the Musée National d'Art Moderne in Paris****), but the *Landscape* that was exhibited is undoubtedly *The Village*,***** painted in Villiers-Adam, between Montmorency and l'Isle-Adam. Like *The Drinkers*, this canvas belonged to Paul Poiret before coming into the possession of Henry Bernstein. The painting, that Segonzac considered one of his best works, was executed with a lighter touch than *The Drinkers*; the palette is somewhat brighter, but still remains basically muted and austere. It was one of the very first landscapes of the Ile-de-France, that had such a profound

---

* See p. 18.   ** See p. 19.   *** See p. 20.   **** See p. 14.   ***** See p. 12.

NOTRE-DAME DE PARIS, 1913. Oil on canvas, 29″ × 39½″ (73.7 × 103 cm)
Collection: Dr and Mrs Howard Sirak, Columbus, Ohio

SPRINGTIME (CHAVILLE), 1920. Oil on canvas, $35\,^1/_{16}'' \times 45\,^5/_8''$ (89×116 cm)
Musée National d'Art Moderne. Centre National d'Art et de Culture Georges Pompidou, Paris

THE BATHERS (THE COUPLE), 1922. Oil on canvas, $68\,^1/_8''\times59\,^{13}/_{16}''$ (173 × 150 cm)
Musée National d'Art Moderne. Centre National d'Art et de Culture Georges Pompidou, Paris

STILL LIFE WITH A CABBAGE, 1919–1920
Oil on canvas, 28¾″ × 36¼″ (73 × 92 cm). The Tate Gallery, London

STILL LIFE (PITCHER, SOUP TUREEN, CARROTS), c. 1923
Oil on canvas, 28¾″ × 36¼″ (73 × 92 cm). Private collection, Paris

The Sleepers, c. 1922–1924. Oil on canvas, $19\,^{11}/_{16}''\times39\,^{3}/_{8}''$ (50 × 100 cm) Musées Nationaux, France. Gift of Pierre Lévy

The Road to Saint-Nom, 1922. Oil on canvas, 36″ × 28¾″ (91.4 × 73 cm)
The Metropolitan Museum of Art, New York. Gift of Sam Salz

THE FARM ON THE ESTATE, 1923.   Oil on canvas, 23⅝″ × 36⅜″ (60 × 93,3)
The Tate Gallery, London

36

SAINT-TROPEZ, 1926. Pen and watercolor on paper, 18½″ × 24″ (47 × 61 cm)
Musée National d'Art Moderne. Centre National d'Art et de Culture Georges Pompidou, Paris

The Uppercut that Missed, c. 1920–1925
Pen, black ink and wash on paper, 10¼″ × 13″ (26 × 33 cm)
Private collection, Paris

appeal for the artist, the region where he was born and that he never ceased to paint throughout his life. The clear-cut structure and orderly vision of *The Village* suggest an ever greater attention was being paid to the experiments of the Cubists, the object of passionate controversies in which, for a time, Segonzac would become embroiled.

Without attempting to give all the details and to resolve all the chronological disputes, we find it useful to recall that the different phases in the history of Cubism, beginning in 1907, paralleled the dates of the first stages of development of Segonzac's art. Picasso painted *The Demoiselles of Avignon* in 1907; the meeting of Picasso and Braque took place the same year, and was followed shortly afterward by the formation of the Groupe du Bateau-Lavoir, which included Picasso, Braque, Max Jacob, Marie Laurencin, Guillaume Apollinaire, André Salmon, Juan Gris, Léger, Delaunay, Gleizes, Le Fauconnier, Lhote, Metzinger, Picabia, Archipenko, La Fresnaye, and the three Duchamp brothers: Jacques Villon, Duchamp-Villon, and Marcel Duchamp. After that came the group known as the Groupe de Puteaux, formed around Jacques Villon, and including Léger, Gleizes, La Fresnaye, Metzinger, Picabia, and Kupka. It is not clear at precisely what moment and in what circumstances Segonzac became associated with this group. (Perhaps it was through his relationship with the circle that revolved around Paul Poiret.) What is known is that in the Salon d'Automne of 1911, a canvas of Segonzac's, *Boxing Match*, was shown in the famous Room VIII, where the Cubists were reassembled. This move was the sequel to a first attempt to group them together in the Salon des Indépendants the previous spring, when, exercising pressure on the committee, Le Fauconnier, Léger, Delaunay, Metzinger, Gleizes, and Marie Laurencin had succeeded in all being shown in Room 41; in that Salon, Segonzac, along with Lhote and Luc-Albert Moreau, had been exhibited in an adjacent room. Albert Gleizes analyzed the situation in the Salon d'Automne of 1911 very well («Bandeaux d'Or,» November 1911): «First of all there were those who, according to whatever criteria, were considered Cubists: Jean Metzinger, Le Fauconnier, Fernand Léger [as well as Gleizes himself]; then those who originally had similar concerns: La Fresnaye, Dunoyer de Segonzac and Luc-Albert Moreau; and finally, thanks to a certain mutuality of interests, André Lhote. Trying to determine as accurately as possible what standards have limited inclusion, I shall search out, scattered in the other rooms, artists who might well have found wall space here, such as Marie Laurencin, Marchand, and Othon Friesz, who have been sacrificed on the altar of who knows what mysterious considerations. The utter lack of comprehension of a yapping press, bewildered by the suddenness with which the movement has taken off and threatening to shoot to earth the highest ambitions of the Impressionists, has managed to impart considerable vitality to the group.»

The press that was the target of Gleizes remarks offered an example of its ineptitude in the person of Louis Vauxcelles («Gil Blas,» September 11, 1930), who observed: «The mad arabesques of Segonzac, who has in other instances given us spirited and lively pen drawings.» The allied camp was not always without reservations and, like André Salmon («Paris-Journal,» September 30, 1911), took care to point out: «Dunoyer de Segonzac and Moreau are merely cousins of the Cubists. Will they join the school of the Cubist artists, or will they all soon foregather at some crossroads? The *Boxing Match* by Dunoyer de Segonzac has a certain proud savagery; in his coloring this artist is related to Moreau, more voluptuously sad and, as someone has quite properly said, Baudelairean.» (This allusion is to an article by Apollinaire that discussed the preceding Salon des Indépendants in «L'Intransigeant,» April 21, 1911.)

Guillaume Apollinaire was somewhat more vague when he wrote («L'Intransigeant,» October 10, 1911): «In a very small room, Room 8, where have been brought together the works of several painters categorized under the general heading of Cubists. . . . [He mentioned Metzinger, Gleizes, Léger, Le Fauconnier, La Fresnaye, Segonzac, L. A. Moreau, and Lhote.] Here is the

NOTRE-DAME (PONT SULLY), undated. Watercolor, 19¾″ × 29½″ (50.2 × 75 cm)
Collection: Mrs Sam Salz, New York

40

powerful *Boxing Match* by Dunoyer de Segonzac, whose palette and technique are making notable progress.» In this article, Gleizes likewise wrote: «I would reproach Dunoyer de Segonzac for the slightly caricatural style he employs in his *Boxers*; I am bothered by some of the exaggeration he uses to heighten the decorative effect. The gray color, although very appealing, lacks variety because it merges too quickly with the flat surfaces of the total composition. I confess that I miss the very superior *Nudes* of the Indépendants. The drawings of Isadora give positive proof of the keenness of his observation; yet he should be on guard against his own enormous facility, for it serves him well when he makes curious notations on a reduced scale, but is not enough to sustain the visual impact of a larger picture. This is perhaps the weakness of the canvas exhibited here, with its overstated realism.» We are familiar with this *Boxing Match** only through a photograph reproduced in 1922, in a monograph by René-Jean for, according to available information, Segonzac destroyed it, an extremely significant fact. The subject, an original one, was inspired by the boxing matches, very popular at the time, that the artist attended regularly from 1910 on. He was fascinated as a spectator by the precision and rapidity of the boxers' moves. The preparatory pen drawings, executed from life on the scene on the spur of the moment — as had been the case earlier with the sketches inspired by the dance, now served to pave the way for a curious composition in which the human form was forced to bend into elliptical curves and was bizarrely deformed (recalling some sculptures by Archipenko). Gleizes very perceptively analyzed the difficulty in passing from the rapid notations of a drawing to the more elaborate conception of an oil painting; this was indeed constantly discernible in the artist's work. The same drawings were used once more after the war, in 1922, to illustrate the «Picture of Boxing» by Tristan Bernard. Toward the end of 1912, *Boxing Match* was exhibited in Berlin alongside works by Braque, Despiau, Vlaminck, Friesz, Gris, Herbin, Kisling, Lhote, Picasso, and others.

Segonzac's interest in the experiments of the Cubists, or at least his awareness that he was part of a similar avant-garde movement, was confirmed by his participation in the exhibition of the Norman Society of Modern Painting, 4 rue Tronchet, where the artists shown included Archipenko, Desvallières, the three Duchamp brothers, Dufy, Friesz, Girieud, Gleizes, La Fresnaye, Marie Laurencin, Le Fauconnier, Léger, Lhote, Marchand, Metzinger, Nadelman, and Picabia. René-Jean («Chronique des Arts»), took note of a landscape by Segonzac, while Gustave Kahn wrote («Mercure de France,» October 16, 1911): «The painters shown are not all Cubists, but some of them are, and those who are not Cubists are bold innovators who seek to achieve some sort of artistic synthesis.... They are all friendly neighbors operating in a spirit of youthful paradox.... Mr. de La Fresnaye and Mr. de Segonzac culled various aspects of Cubism and used these variations effectively in their own work.»

The «kinship» with Cubism (to borrow Salmon's term), clearly apparent in 1911, continued in 1912. The *Still Life (Venus de Medici),*** which was exhibited at the Salon des Indépendants in 1912, showed very plainly the appeal exerted by Cubism, particularly when it came to the organization of forms. The Salon des Indépendants of 1912 revived the controversy that focused on Cubism. Louis Vauxcelles («Gil Blas,» March 19, 1912), who fulminated against «Ubu-Kub,» merely mentioned «the curious experimentation with volume and the dirty colors» of Segonzac in his comments on Room XIX, where the painter was exhibiting with Alix, Marie Laurencin, Fauconnet, Mainssieux, La Fresnaye and Vlaminck. Taking an opposite position, André Salmon wrote in «Paris-Journal,» (March 19, 1912), apropos of the same room: «One of the finest pictures in this delightful room is a still life by Dunoyer de Segonzac, *Venus in Plaster*,

---

* See p. 22.   ** See p. 11.

STILL LIFE: BOUQUET IN FRONT OF THE WINDOW, c. 1925–1930
Watercolor, 20⁷/₁₆″ × 25¹/₄″ (52 × 64 cm). Private collection, Paris

STILL LIFE WITH BLACK BASKET, c. 1925–1930. Watercolor, 24⁷/₁₆″ × 18¹/₂″ (62 × 47 cm)
Private collection, Paris

Three Trees, 1922. Pen and gray wash on paper, 11¹³/₁₆″ × 18⁷/₈″ (30 × 48 cm)
Musée du Louvre, Cabinet des Dessins, Paris

44

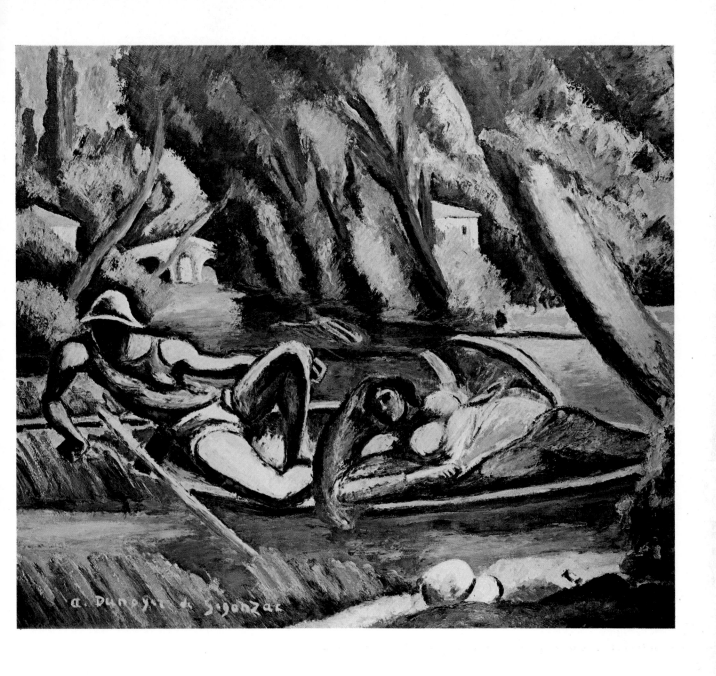

THE ROWERS, 1924. Oil on canvas, $78\,^3/_4'' \times 82\,^{11}/_{16}''$ (200×210 cm)
Private collection, Switzerland

BACCHUS, 1927. Oil on canvas, $25\frac{5}{8}'' \times 31\frac{7}{8}''$ (65 × 81 cm)
Musée National d'Art Moderne. Centre National d'Art et de Culture Georges Pompidou, Paris

THE SEATED BATHER, 1927. Oil on canvas, 31⅞″ × 39⅜″ (81 × 100 cm)
Private collection, Paris

THE FARM AT AIRE, 1925. Oil on canvas, $13\,^{3}/_{4}''\times30\,^{11}/_{16}''$ (35 × 78 cm)
Musée National d'Art Moderne. Centre National d'Art et de Culture Georges Pompidou, Paris

épreuve d'essai   à Dunoyer de Segonzac

San MacVea an his Seconds, 1922. Etching, 9¾″ × 7¾″ (24.8 × 19.8 cm)
Bibliothèque Nationale, Paris

*Berthe Undressing; Engraving from Bubu de Montparnasse by Charles-Louis Philippe,
engraved and published in 1929. Bibliothèque Nationale, Paris*

Study for the «Springtime in the Suburbs», 1922
Pen and light gray wash on paper, 11¹³/₁₆″ × 18¹/₁₆″ (30 × 46 cm)
Private collection, Paris

bathed in a subdued light that brightens a sheaf of foliage like a misprized aureole.» Apollinaire's comments («L'Intransigeant,» April 3, 1912) about this same work were equally lyrical: «L. A. Moreau . . . paints bodies of extreme languor . . . and as sad as love itself. This *mot juste* from an admirable sonnet by Théodore de Banville might well be repeated when viewing Segonzac's still life, *Venus in Plaster*, in which light artfully plays on forms that revive the Beauty that followed the road of Paros and the Antiquity that still quivers beneath the heap of ruins.» I should like also to quote the opinions of two critics who were favorable, but who were far less deeply involved in the movement. The comment of Roger-Marx («Chronique des Arts,» March 23, 1912) included: «The less dogmatic, less stilted works of Mr. de La Fresnaye and Mr. de Segonzac . . . have their origins in Cubism, but are already emancipated from its strictures.» Gustave Kahn wrote almost the same thing in the «Mercure de France» (April 1, 1912): «The *Venus in Plaster* of Mr. de Segonzac possesses great charm. Because the influence of Cubism on the artist has become diluted, we are able to perceive that he has all the requisites to be an excellent painter.» Segonzac's position was thought to be marginal in comparison with that of the pure theoreticians, but in the eyes of the public and contemporary critics, his efforts seemed to be impossible to explain except as they related to the Cubist dogma. Immediately after the Indépendants, Segonzac participated in a group show in the offices of the periodical «La Vie,» 68 rue Mazarine; among the other exhibitors, we should like to call attention to Bouche and Luc-Albert Moreau.

His submission to the Salon d'Automne that same year was well received, notably by Apollinaire («L'Intransigeant,» October 1, 1912), who praised «the landscapes without affectation of Mr. Dunoyer de Segonzac, a painter of biting honesty.»

In October 1912, Segonzac took part in one of the most important public displays by the Cubists, the famous Salon de la Section d'Or at the Galerie La Boétie. He contributed two works, a *Group of Nudes* and a *Still Life*, that were hung near those of the three Duchamp brothers, Gleizes, Gris, La Fresnaye, Marie Laurencin, Léger, Lhote, Marchand, Metzinger, Picabia, and the sculptures of Archipenko. And yet, neither Gleizes nor Metzinger in their book entitled «About Cubism,» published in 1912, nor Apollinaire in «Cubist Painters,» published in 1913, made any mention of Segonzac.

At the end of 1912, he was invited to participate in a group show at the Galerie Druet; it was utterly eclectic, as demonstrated by the fact that it brought together Maurice Denis, Laprade, Maillol, Redon, Sérusier, Vallotton, Valtat, and Van Rysselberghe. Two reviews of this exhibition deserve special notice. The first was by René-Jean, author of the preface for Segonzac's first one-man show in 1914, who also would be the first to devote a monograph to the artist. His article appeared in the «Chronique des Arts,» December 7, 1912: «The art of Mr. Dunoyer de Segonzac, one of the most gifted of our young painters, is related to the movement that culminated in the exaggerations of "Cubism." With a solid construction that is remarkable and a talent for synthesis that would be admirably suited to sculpture, he has painted with manifest joy landscapes and still lifes, profoundly harmonious, in which grays that remind one of Corot predominate.» An article by Gustave Kahn in the «Mercure de France» on December 16, 1912, although somewhat more critical, defines the artist's major characteristics fairly accurately: «Mr. de Segonzac is an extremely interesting artist who skirts on the border of Cubism; he has aesthetic talent, sincerity and a sense of order, but his technique tends to lack variety. His experimentation with volume renders somewhat monotonous the landscapes, the pasture lands, the village streets, the ponds, that are nevertheless appealing, with their very pretty, velvety tones. A still life with a goddess in plaster provides a varied replication of a picture exhibited by Mr. de Segonzac last year, and that marked the first public success of Cubism.»

Two Leaning Trees, 1926. Oil on canvas, 32″ × 25¾″ (81.5 × 65.5 cm)
Collection: Mrs Sam Salz, New York

«La Côte de Bœuf» (Rib of Beef), c. 1930. Oil on canvas, 13″ × 21⅝″ (33 × 55 cm)
Collection: Mr and Mrs David Evins, New York

STILL LIFE WITH SOUP TUREEN, c. 1930.   Oil on canvas, 21⅝″ × 31½″ (55 × 80 cm)
Collection: Jerome K. Ohrbach, Beverly Hills, California

THE MILL AT QUINTEJOIE, c. 1935. Oil on canvas, 32″ × 24″ (81.3 × 59.7 cm)
Collection: Mrs Jane Robinson, Sidney, Beverly Hills, California

1913 showed a distinct and obvious evolution in Segonzac's work. His growth is evident in such paintings as *Still Life*, now in Copenhagen, or *Fancy Breadloaves* (known as *The Picnic*),* now in Paris, at the Musée National d'Art Moderne. One discovers in *Fancy Breadloaves* a careful construction reminiscent of the surprising technique of *The Drinkers* of 1910. Layers of paint are superimposed one on top of the other and provide a balance for one another. Once more Segonzac makes use of a dark palette, replete with warm colors, that is very different from the grays and beiges of the *Venus de Medici*.** These indications that the artist was relying anew on the wellsprings that were uniquely his, signs more easily discerned from the perspective of elapsed time, were immediately recognized by the most perspicacious of his contemporaries. Roger-Marx («Chronique des Arts,» March 22, 1913), recalling the works of Segonzac, and at the same time those of Marchand and Luc-Albert Moreau, spoke of pictures «ripened and matured at leisure, created by men in full possession of their powers, in which a perfect tone accurately stresses the overall surface.» He continued: «I am aware of the extent to which such works link up with our artistic traditions; yet without "Cubism," would we now have them to enjoy?» Apollinaire did not conceal a certain disappointment («Montjoie,» March 18, 1913): «In lieu of a calling card, Dunoyer de Segonzac sends us a jug and other objects. It is an unpretentious gift from a painter who knows how to be audacious and proved it three years ago, when he exhibited *The Confinement*, a canvas that we should appreciate seeing again.» He had the same attitude toward the work submitted by the painter to the Salon d'Automne («L'Intransigeant,» November 15, 1913): «*Summer*, by Dunoyer de Segonzac, employs a whole gamut of somber shades and flaunts a disdain for easy popularity that is admirable. Thus he appears to have returned to his point of departure, *The Confinement*, done four years ago, a bold and austere painting.» Apollinaire was undoubtedly alluding to a picture exhibited at the Indépendants, possibly in 1910, possibly in 1911; as we have already indicated, some of his paintings are difficult to identify. *Summer*, mentioned previously, presents the same difficulty; according to Roger Allard, who referred to this work on several occasions («Les Ecrits Français,» November and December 1913): «It evokes for us an "Illumination" of Arthur Rimbaud. The shadowy freshness, the explosive energy and the dark vigor of the burningly hot season is expressed through the utilization of very simple subjects, skillfully selected.» It should be noted that Roger Allard professed a profound admiration for Segonzac's art, on which he commented in an article that became especially well known because it was featured in the almanac of the Blaue Reiter. Nevertheless, even though this was considered as an established fact in the monograph of René-Jean, we have been unable to discover any confirmation of the supposition that Segonzac participated in any of the exhibitions of the Blaue Reiter. However, given the artists with whom Segonzac was friendly at the time, such participation in one of the most important avant-garde movements in Europe would have been entirely plausible.

Toward the end of 1913, Segonzac's famous *Boxing Match* was featured in a somewhat unusual exhibition at the Doré Galleries in London entitled «Post-Impressionist and Futurist Exhibition.» In it, Bonnard, Van Gogh, Gauguin, and Signac kept company with Brancusi, Camoin, Picasso, Derain, Matisse, Lhote, Severini, and several English artists. However, in that same year, the outstanding event for Segonzac was his participation in the sensational Armory Show. In February 1913, in New York, a vast exhibition opened, of more than a thousand items, organized by the Association of American Painters and Sculptors, entitled «International Exhibition of Modern Art,» which later became known as the Armory Show (from the name of the building that housed it in New York and that served as an arsenal for an

---

* See p. 13.   ** See p. 11.

infantry regiment). On the poster announcing it, Segonzac's name appeared at the bottom of a list of prestigious artists, on which the mere names of Delacroix, Ingres, Cézanne, all the Impressionists, Gauguin, Van Gogh, Seurat, Signac, Lautrec, Braque, Dufy, and more, not to mention numerous sculptors, are enough to suggest the scope and importance of this exhibition. Segonzac showed six paintings in New York (landscapes, *Pasture Scenes*, a *Bucolic*) and some drawings; some of them were shipped to Chicago, then to Boston, with the rest of the exhibition. Among the initiators of this ambitious enterprise, which can be numbered among the most significant happenings in the history of prewar art, was an attorney and collector, John Quinn, who bought many of the works exhibited at the Armory Show and was one of the first in the United States to purchase any of Segonzac's output (notably a *Notre-Dame de Paris,* * painted in 1913, executed in the colors of brown lava). At a later date Quinn was to donate to the French government Seurat's *The Circus*; the rest of the collection, including Douanier Rousseau's *Sleeping Gypsy*, was sold in Paris in 1926. It was also on the occasion of the Armory Show that another distinguished American collector purchased some of Segonzac's works; his name was Arthur Jerome Eddy, a Chicago attorney who in 1913 bequeathed quite a few works to the Chicago Art Institute (his portrait by Whistler, 1894, and a series by Kandinsky). In «Cubists and Post-Impressionism,» published in London in 1915, A. J. Eddy reproduced several paintings by Segonzac, whom he described as a «virile Impressionist!» At the beginning of 1914, Segonzac had his first one-man show at the Galerie Levesque, 109 rue du Faubourg Saint-Honoré, that would later become the Galerie Barbazanges, then the Galerie Georges Bernheim. This exhibition, which featured *The Village, The Drinkers*, and the *Venus de Medici*, seems almost like a sort of reflection on five years of painting. (The earliest of the works shown date from 1909.) The catalogue had a preface by René-Jean, who pinpointed accurately the ground Segonzac had covered artistically: «The road he has followed has had no detours. He has gone along it without the least divergence. Between a particular still life, executed five years ago, and another created yesterday, the only difference that exists is a somewhat greater suppleness, a skill that moves the viewer more, in the recent picture. He belongs to a generation that will loom large in any history of the evolution of painting.» Reception by the critics was generally favorable. The most lavish praise was heaped on the young artist by Louis Vauxcelles («Gil Blas,» February 5, 1914): «The ordeal of a complete exhibition is always a grueling one for a young artist. . . . Mr. Dunoyer de Segonzac passes the test with flying colors. The position of Mr. de Segonzac in the young artists' school is a quite special one. He is among those who, wishing to create, do not feel a need [as my colleague and friend, René-Jean, has observed in his remarkable preface] to walk in the unfortunate path of those who allow cold theory to predominate over emotion.» (That is, the Cubists.) The laudatory lines written by Roger Allard («Les Ecrits Français,» March 5, 1914) compensated fully for the unfriendly criticism: «Like so many others, Segonzac might have adhered to Cubism as some people fly airplanes, because that calling is fashionable today. He has preferred to develop in depth a personal and individual style whose vigorous amplitude is attested to by this fine exhibition . . . and that we should like to see flourishing freely in the new works that we can surely await confidently.» However, the aesthetic quality of Segonzac's art was not acknowledged by everyone, as is demonstrated by the ironic criticism of Louis Hautecœur, who would eventually change his opinion («Chronique des Arts,» February 14, 1914): «At the risk of being taken for a "Philistine," a "bourgeois," a "grocery clerk," . . . we wonder if the effects legitimize the scorn of natural and no doubt conventional forms. . . . The exhibition as a whole can only cause us to regret that the painter's genuine gifts have been wasted in the service of vain and foolish theories.»

---

* See p. 29.

«The Grape Trellis» by Colette, 1932. Etching. Bibliothèque Nationale, Paris

Ploughed Land, c. 1935–1937.   Pen and gray wash on paper, 11⁷/₈″ × 18⁹/₁₆″ (30.1 × 47.2 cm)
Musée National d'Art Moderne. Centre National d'Art et de Culture Georges Pompidou, Paris

THE CHURCH AT COUILLY, c. 1930. Oil on canvas, 25⅝″ × 39⅜″ (65 × 100 cm)
Musée National d'Art Moderne. Centre National d'Art et de Culture Georges Pompidou, Paris

STILL LIFE WITH BASKET, 1936. Oil on canvas, 39⅜″ × 31⅞″ (100 × 81 cm)
Musées Nationaux, France. Gift of Pierre Lévy

FIVE EGGS IN A BOWL, c. 1950. Oil on panel, 10⅝″ × 13¾″ (27 × 35 cm)
Private collection, Paris

THE SOUP TUREEN OF MOUSTIERS, c. 1938–1939.   Oil on canvas, 31⅞″ × 25⅝″ (81 × 65 cm)
Museum of Modern Art, Teheran

STILL LIFE WITH WINE GLASS, c. 1936. Oil on canvas, 31⅞″ × 25⅝″ (81 × 65 cm)
Musée d'Art Moderne de la Ville de Paris

SAINT-TROPEZ, SEEN FROM THE CITADEL, c. 1950
Pen and watercolor on paper, 21¾″ × 29½″ (55 × 75 cm)
Musée de l'Annonciade, Saint-Tropez, France

THE BEACH AT SAINT-TROPEZ, c. 1936
Oil on canvas, $25\,{}^{13}/_{16}''\times39\,{}^{3}/_{8}''$ (65.5 × 100 cm)
Musée National d'Art Moderne. Centre National d'Art et de Culture Georges Pompidou, Paris

STILL LIFE (GLADIOLAS), c. 1936. Oil on canvas, 24¼″ × 31½″ (61.5 × 80 cm)
Collection: Mrs Sam Salz, New York

69

THE CHAPEL AT VERSAILLES, c. 1946. Watercolor, $19\,^{5}/_{16}{}''\times25\,^{1}/_{4}{}''$ (49 × 64 cm)
Musée Lambinet, Versailles, France

LANDSCAPE, THE «MAURES», c. 1935–1940
Pen and watercolor on paper, 17¹/₈" × 24⁷/₁₆" (43.5 × 62 cm)
Musée National d'Art Moderne. Centre National d'Art et de Culture Georges Pompidou, Paris

Engraving for the Georgics by Virgil, 1927 till 1947. Bibliothèque Nationale, Paris

THE POND OF VILLE D'AVRAY IN WINTERTIME, 1937
Pen and watercolor on paper, 21$^{7}/_{16}''$ × 29$^{5}/_{16}''$ (54.5 × 74.5 cm)
Musée National d'Art Moderne. Centre National d'Art et de Culture Georges Pompidou, Paris

It is fortunate that, before the war broke out, Segonzac was able to put on display the sum total of his efforts. From that time on, the artistic itinerary of the painter appears to have been carefully laid out. This is especially true of all the subjects tackled by the artist: compositions with figures in a landscape, landscapes of the Ile-de-France, and still lifes, which planted the seeds for future development. His pictorial and personal technique, which simultaneously points up both his perfect mastery and his potential difficulties, was already established. One last time we should like to quote Apollinaire, who, even though he was disappointed in Segonzac's evolution («L'Intransigeant,» March 25, 1913, November 15, 1913, and March 3, 1914), paid the artist admiring homage («Paris-Journal,» June 21, 1914): «The Luxembourg Museum has no Seurat, almost no Cézanne. Guys, Lautrec, and Gauguin are, in a manner of speaking, really not represented. It does not have on display any of the works that make up the vital art of the last few years — no Matisse, no Picasso, no Derain, no Braque, no Laurencin, no Picabia, no Delaunay, no Dunoyer de Segonzac, no Metzinger, no Gleizes, no Henri Rousseau, no Friesz, no Vallotton, no Guérin, no Manguin.»

THE WAR (1914–1918)

Segonzac was in Saint-Tropez when he learned about the declaration of war. He rejoined his unit in Fontainebleau as an infantry sergeant. He took part in the fierce battles that took place in the region of Nancy, then, later, in those at Bois-Le-Prêtre. Like a number of other painters, notably Braque and Villon, he was subsequently transferred to the camouflage section, created by Guirand de Scevola. Maurice Denis, who met Segonzac when he himself was a painter for the army, in his «Diary» (October 11–29, 1917), gave a sympathetic picture of the «handsome visage of Segonzac, a true leader, good and gay,» who at the time happened to be in the region of Noyon, along with Boussingault, Camoin, Girieud, and La Fresnaye, who was working on theatre sets for a revue of his unit. Evidently the war meant to Segonzac an interruption of his work for four years, during a crucial period of his evolution. He had barely reached his thirtieth year. Nevertheless, his immediate reaction was to translate into graphic terms the experiences he had lived through at the front. The admirable drawings, hachured, sketched, and executed in the trenches and the military camps, are among the most moving, the most free of rhetoric, of the body of testimony concerning World War I. What he observed in the war was not so much the formidable power of its destructive weapons as the suffering of the infantryman squatting in a trench, the wounded being brought back, the soldiers delousing themselves, the cook of the cantonment. In 1915–1916 he stayed for a while in a camp of aviators, the «Camp of Storks,» in Breuil-le-Sec, near Clermont-Oise, where he did drawings of the airplanes of Védrines and Guynemer. The war drawings quickly became known. Some of them were published as early as 1915 in «L'Elan» of Ozenfant and «Le Crapouillot»; others were shown in the Galerie Marseille, 16 rue de Seine, at the beginning of 1917 and at the end of 1918. Moreover, in December 1917 this same gallery exhibited on its walls a joint show by Dunoyer de Segonzac, La Fresnaye, Luc-Albert Moreau, Boussingault, Camoin, Dufresne, Marchand, and others. Segonzac did make use of his drawings, which were sometimes highlighted by touches of watercolor, in his painted compositions. However, these sketches were the beneficiary of an unexpected development that undoubtedly was responsible for them becoming more widely known.* Indeed, once the war was over, following the advice of the bibliophile René Blum, Segonzac undertook in 1919 to illustrate

---

* See p. 27.

74

Engraving for the Georgics by Virgil, 1927 till 1947. Bibliothèque Nationale, Paris

THE COUNTRYSIDE AT VILLEPREUX IN JUNE, 1945
Pen and watercolor on paper, 22¾″ × 29⅛″ (58 × 74 cm)
Musée National d'Art Moderne. Centre National d'Art et de Culture Georges Pompidou, Paris

«The Wooden Crosses» by Roland Dorgelès, a book published in 1921. It was in order to bring this project to fruition that Segonzac, who had learned the basics of etching from a session with J. E. Laboureur, first directed his efforts to engraving. Thus were born the first attempts of what was eventually to be a fairly large output of engravings (the catalogue raisonné lists no less than sixteen hundred such pieces), which are among the most significant of the twentieth century. He was already concerned with book illustration, a genre in which he excelled and about which he observed, in an introduction to the exhibition of his engravings in Vichy in 1971: «I have always thought that the illustration of a book is less a graphic and literal commentary on a text than a work that parallels the written word, which should express the essence of its spirit and create an appropriate ambience.» «The Wooden Crosses,» together with «The Ball of Mistletoe» and «Cabaret of the Beautiful Woman,» also by Dorgelès and illustrated with Segonzac engravings, published respectively in 1921, 1922, and 1924, are magnificent evidence that this definition is valid. Some variations and pieces not used in «The Wooden Crosses» were issued in 1926 under the title «Eight War Illustrations.»

1920–1925

As soon as he was demobilized, Dunoyer de Segonzac took up residence in the house his family owned in Chaville, at the same time retaining his studio in Paris. Although he devoted part of his time to engravings, illustrating the trilogy by Dorgelès, as well as «Picture of Boxing» by Tristan Bernard,* published by the «Nouvelle Revue Française» in 1922, he never ceased to paint. As a matter of fact, the years from 1920 to 1925 would even be among the most productive of his career as a painter. The principal subjects treated in the course of these years were landscapes, in which austere scenes of the Ile-de-France predominate, still lifes, and large compositions with figures centering around such topics as *Rowers* or *Springtime in the Suburbs*.**

From 1919 on, Segonzac once more exhibited at the Salon d'Automne, then, at the beginning of 1920, at the Indépendants. The Salon d'Automne of 1920 featured a landscape entitled *Springtime*,*** painted in Chaville. The identification of this painting can be confirmed by the reproduction in «Amour de l'Art,» a prestigious periodical that would publish, in May 1921, a brilliant and detailed study devoted to the artist by Claude Roger-Marx. In this painting, there is renewed application of the thick, well-worked paint of the prewar period; yet the palette, although severe, has nevertheless subtler shadings and lighter coloring. This canvas, almost abstract in its overall appearance, reflects a sure intuition and an innate feeling for the partition of masses. Segonzac's art during this period invariably places itself outside the main currents of other contemporary movements, thanks to an originality that seems to have little interest in pleasing at first blush. The somber landscapes of this era, such as *Farm on the Estate*,**** painted in Serbonne, near Crécy-en-Brie, about 1923 and *The Road to Saint-Nom*,***** also painted around 1923, occasionally show an Expressionist influence that is quite unexpected. One could equally well cite *Landscape at Villepreux* (sometimes entitled *The Two Trees*), in the collection of Pierre Lévy of Troyes. The tortured, almost tragic aspect of the paintings is much less evident in the contemporary drawings and engravings with similar themes. This is especially true of the famous series of etchings that are known under the name of *Suite* or *Landscapes of Morin*, issued in 1923 and evoking the region of Serbonne, Villiers-sur-Morin and Crécy-en-Brie, where the artist stayed

---

* See also Sam MacVea, p. 49. ** See p. 51. *** See p. 30. **** See p. 36. ***** See p. 35.

in 1923–1924. The same comments could be made about the plates engraved in Chaville and Versailles in 1924. All the motifs of the Valley of Morin, Chaville, Versailles, and Marly, which should be added to those of the banks of the Yerres* treated before the war, would be taken up anew in the years that followed.

These engravings, executed directly from life, although their formats were often impressively large, appear to be a sort of poetic divertissement that paralleled the eclectic work he was doing in painting. In them, his strokes followed the whims of his hand and eye. He very effectively transposed into a graphic rendition the atmosphere of an Ile-de-France that was like a great park with noble trees, with a village church steeple appearing behind the trees in a valley. Segonzac immediately adopted the technique of etching, which demands the fewest restraints and, from the point of view of the effect it produces, is the closest to drawing with a pen. The artist simply draws on a copperplate, varnished in advance, with a pointed instrument, thus baring the metal, which can then be washed in a more or less prolonged acid bath. The chemical process thus makes ready the hollows that will hold the printing ink. This technique is marvelously well suited to the sketcher's spontaneous efforts, as, at the beginning of his career, the pages devoted to the dance have revealed to us.

The landscapes and nudes engraved between 1920 and 1925, so very different from his contemporary oil paintings, mark a new stage in Segonzac's development. Segonzac was aware of the difficulties entailed in his pictorial technique as well as of the fact that etching was a means of expression perfectly suited to his experimentation. He began to give priority to engraving over painting; as he was simplifying his painting technique, he was perfecting and increasing his work in the field of engraving.

As a counterpart to these landscapes, Segonzac painted still lifes** that resembled them in the thickness of the paint and in the gamut of colors. The objects depicted were crude and simple (bread, a stoneware jug, a white soup tureen, a bottle, vegetables), were simply placed on a kitchen table, and stand out against a neutral background. All the familiar elements can be found again and again in each of the still lifes. Segonzac's special technique seems gradually to give tangible form to them as if they were modeled in relief. The thickness of the paint appears to reflect a direct transposition of the subject, as his landscapes, done in earth tones, appear to be the concrete expression of the reality they describe.

During those same years, Segonzac gave indications of his ambition to paint large compositions enlivened by human figures. *The Bathers, The Sleepers,*** *Rowers*, and *Young Women of the Marne* inevitably evoke, because of their subject matter, *Young Women on the Bank of the Seine* by Courbet and *The Picnic* by Manet. Moreover, the large formats that the painter selected for these paintings make this comparison — suggested by the titles chosen by Segonzac — still easier to accept. These allusions testify very clearly to the painter's desire to have his work judged in the context of the accomplishments of his elders, while at the same time he was bringing a new and personal spirit to classical themes. All these compositions treat anew several well-defined types, combined in different ways, and preceded by numerous preparatory pen drawings. *Nude with a Newspaper*, a female nude, extremely foreshortened and lacking a head, is to be found both in a canvas in the Tate Gallery in London, dated by the artist as executed in 1922–1923, in another canvas of the Musée National d'Art Moderne in Paris, and in a large composition, also in the Musée National d'Art Moderne, entitled *The Bathers* (or *The Couple*),**** that was almost certainly exhibited at the Salon d'Automne of 1922. Other paintings deal with the theme of *Nude with a Black Shoe*, in which the model, who is curled up, is treated as a bizarre

---

* See p. 17.   ** See pp. 32 and 33.   *** See p. 34.   **** See p. 31.

object. (In fact, all the male and female nudes of this period are treated in a similar manner.) The subject of *Springtime* or of *Sunday in the Suburbs*, with a couple, sheltered under a parasol, entwined in an embrace, quite naturally precedes the composition of the huge *Rowers*. This last work is a milestone in the artist's career that is just as important as the landmark status of his first canvases in 1910.

This composition occupied a great deal of the artist's time between 1923 and 1924. We are familiar with two versions, exactly the same size. One, reproduced here, was for a long time part of the collection of Jean-Arthur Fontaine, whereas the other, executed after the first, was acquired for the collection of Jean Patou, the couturier. They were preceded by numerous sketches in oil and watercolor and very elaborate pen drawings, highlighted by washes. Segonzac went into detail (H. Hugault, 1973, p. 100): «*Rowers* was inspired by the spectacle of couples in rowboats whom I observed on the Marne or on the river of Grand-Morin, that I painted and drew from 1924 to 1935. All of the drawings and sketches were executed from life as I observed the spectacle of these young lovers stretched out in boats on the beautiful rivers of the Ile-de-France.» *Rowers** is a perfect example that enables us to follow the progress of the artist from the first rapid drawing, in which he excelled, to the elaborate culmination in an oil painting. In it, the landscape occupies a much more important position than it was given in compositions such as *The Couple* or *The Sleepers*. Finally, the palette, enriched by bright greens and reds, is profoundly different from the monotones, with bases in gray, brown, and ocher, of his earlier works, while the pictorial effect therefore is far lighter and more transparent. The artist attained here the balance and sureness of expression of an accomplished master. After the completion of the series of *Rowers*, Segonzac abandoned this type of large composition, which he would take up again only after 1930, with the subject of *Beaches of Bouillabaisse.*** *Rowers* marks the conclusion of the preceding period and at the same time allows us to foresee the ultimate evolution of a simpler technique, less thickly overlaid, and a more diversified palette. It should be noted that Segonzac, who until 1922 had made regular submissions to the Salon des Indépendants and the Salon d'Automne, refrained from sending entries to these shows for almost fifteen years thereafter. Several one-man exhibitions, in France as well as in foreign countries, were devoted to the artist, most particularly one at the Galerie Barbazanges in Paris in 1924. In London, exhibitions at the Independent Gallery in 1920, 1923, and 1927 were largely responsible for making the painter's work known in Great Britain, where his first aficionados included Percy More Turner, Ivor Spencer Churchill, F. Hindely Smith, Michael Sadler, and Henry Bentinck.

Two events ensured Segonzac's reputation as a famous artist. The first was a sale by Paul Poiret, who was undergoing financial difficulties and offered his collection at auction on November 18, 1925. This collection is famous (it was exhibited at the Galerie Barbazanges in 1917) and known for its avant-garde character. Alongside paintings, drawings, and watercolors by Segonzac, there were works by Picasso, Van Dongen, Dufy, Derain, Picabia, Matisse, and Utrillo. The prices that the works of Segonzac brought astounded the critics: Henry Bernstein paid 67,000 francs for *The Village*; Marseille bought *The Drinkers* for 90,000 francs, while it was whispered abroad that Poiret had purchased it in 1910 for 900 francs. At the time, an offer of almost 100,000 francs for a picture, especially one executed by a living and still youthful artist, was altogether exceptional.

---

* See pp. 6, 7, and 45.   ** See p. 67.

The second event, less sensational but equally significant, was the acquisition in 1926 by the Musée du Luxembourg of a picture by Segonzac, *The Farm at Aire,** painted in Saint-Tropez. The first monographs devoted to the artist were published during this period, one by René-Jean in 1922, one by Claude Roger-Marx in 1925, followed a few years later, in 1929, by one by Paul Jamot. From that time on, Segonzac's fame was assured.

In 1925, the purchase of a property in Saint-Tropez that belonged to Camoin, and of which he became joint owner with his friends Luc-Albert Moreau and Villebœuf, was the occasion for regular and frequent sojourns in the South of France. At a later date, Segonzac bought out his friends' shares and for the rest of his life kept for himself the property, called «Le Maquis,» situated on the road that led to the chapel of Sainte-Anne and that overlooked the bay of Saint-Tropez. The panorama that encircled his house, as well as all the surroundings of Saint-Tropez, supplied the painter with familiar motifs that he developed as a counterpart to the landscapes around Paris, where the artist never failed to work when he was not staying in the South of France.

The growing influence of the light of Provence was supplemented by another discovery, that of the technique of watercolor, which had a definite impact on the artist's work. The first watercolors coincided in date with the first essays in engraving. Indeed, if certain war drawings in pen were already highlighted with touches of color, that did not mean that he was yet achieving the elaborate, fully structured, definitive works that we know as his watercolors. The artist himself carefully made a distinction between his «rapid drawings, underlined by touches of watercolor,» which he executed throughout his life, and his concept of true watercolor, actually «water painting,» done in a technique inspired by oil painting of the sort he had done from the beginning of his career. He particularly emphasized (for the last time in the work devoted to his watercolors that was published after his death in 1976) «the long and laborious work, accomplished in many successive sessions,» which was a characteristic feature of his technique. He described in detail first the preliminary drawing in India ink, highlighted by wash, then several sessions (at least three) spent doing «painting in watercolor ... that constitute three successive stages superimposed on one another,» the first consisting of pure, brilliant tones and forming a very colorful base, which was reworked and made more harmonious during succeeding sessions. The technical details, such as the quality of the paper and the colors employed, also assumed enormous importance in his eyes. Apropos of this, Segonzac recalled that he owed Signac a number of pieces of advice, even though, in certain instances, he did just the opposite of what Signac had counseled, notably when he used raw sienna and ocher, shades that were scorned by Signac and very frequently used by Segonzac. Ochers served primarily to give body and «firmness» (a term, as Claude Roger-Marx pointed out, of which Segonzac was fond) to certain tones and to structure the initial schema of the composition. An old watercolor, such as *Scaffold Poles,*** is still very close to the concept of a pen drawing, very elaborate, highlighted by notations in color that give to the work a density and richness of coloring unequaled in his contemporary oil paintings, and foreshadow the watercolors of his maturity. It is likewise remarkable that the works prior to 1930, such as *Black Basket**** and *Bouquet in Front of the Window,***** display all the characteristics of the works created at the end of the artist's life.

However, it was only subsequent to 1930 that Segonzac adopted a uniform format (about 55×75 centimeters or $21^{5}/_{8}'' \times 29^{1}/_{2}''$), that corresponded to the standard dimensions of the paper he selected. It is difficult to put one's finger on the principal reason for the artist's evolution, apparent from 1925 on. The brilliant introduction of subjects inspired by Saint-Tropez and the

* See p. 48.   ** See p. 24.   *** See p. 43.   **** See p. 42.

THE SEA AND THE MOUNTAIN, 1946
Pen and watercolor on charcoal sketch on paper, 13″ × 28⅛″ (33.5 × 71.5 cm)
Musée National d'Art Moderne. Centre National d'Art et de Culture Georges Pompidou, Paris

surrounding region strikes the viewer at first glance. His use of watercolor certainly modified significantly the technique of his oil paintings, which would no longer have the thick, overlaid quality, extremely exaggerated during 1910–1914 and still very evident in the paintings of 1920–1923. Finally, his discovery of etching, which expanded and enriched his development as a draftsman, was responsible for a radical change in his art.

MATURITY (1925–1950)

The critic Jean-Louis Vaudoyer, writing a review of the Salon des Indépendants for «Le Crapouillot» in 1926, stated that «after Utrillo, those most copied are Picasso, Matisse and Segonzac.» This shows the considerable influence Segonzac exerted on his contemporaries. Yet he exhibited very little and, after 1930, chiefly in foreign countries. His art, restrained, controlled, deeply embedded in reality, easily and harmoniously earned a place on the rolls of a realistic, nonabstract tradition. The success of his work lay precisely in the fact that he expressed so marvelously the aspirations of those who sought to be independent, an attitude still appealing and prevalent today. After 1925, the stylistic evolution of the artist reached a sort of point of equilibrium. The themes he had treated formerly were developed, enriched, adapted to the varied disciplines of the techniques for oil paintings, watercolors, engravings, and, of course, drawings. It is not unusual to find the same themes, figures, or landscapes, using each of these techniques. It is also true that, little by little, Segonzac abandoned oil painting, preferring to work in watercolor.

The landscapes of the South of France, *The Farm at Aire* and *The Gulf of Saint-Tropez,** occupy a prominent place among the pictures produced during this period. The austere, wintry landscapes of the Mediterranean are peopled with figures that re-create an aura of ancient mythology. *The Seated Bather*** of 1927, which evokes Greek athletes, introduced this series, of which the *Bacchus**** of 1933 is a more explicit representation. As a counterpart to these male nudes, Segonzac painted a whole series of *Female Bathers*, for which models came to pose, without embarrassment, on a little artificial beach that the artist had had set up. These nudes nonchalantly stretched out under the sun were named *Antiope***** and *Ceres*, and would find a permanent home in the illustrations of Virgil's «Georgics,» in which Segonzac was beginning to be interested.

The beaches of 1927–1928 were also the subject of a series of engravings, published by the artist, and some drawings would be used later on as illustrations for a text by Léon-Paul Fargue, «Burning Coasts.» One should not forget that it was at this period that people started to discover the pleasures of «dolce far niente» in the summer sun of the Côte d'Azur, a region that, until that time, had been frequented exclusively during the winter. Thus Segonzac truly made himself the chronicler of his times. Another series by Segonzac, evoking the beaches of the Côte d'Azur, was issued in 1934. The muted tones of the oil paintings (the bluish green of the olive trees, the ocher, the brown of the flesh tints, the ice blue of the sea) become livelier in the watercolors, and their effect is further enhanced by the brightness of the white paper. Nevertheless, the watercolors, like the canvases, reflect a consistent vision, a consistent desire to achieve a structured composition. After 1930, a certain transparency in the layers of oil paint, a direct result of his activity as a watercolorist, became very pronounced. The landscapes of Provence, which are to

---

* See p. 37.   ** See p. 47.   *** See p. 46.   **** See p. 69.

be numbered among the artist's masterpieces, are still on a par with the work Segonzac was pursuing in the vicinity of Paris. Whether they be oil paintings or watercolors, we find in them the old familiar themes: *The Church at Couilly,** in the valley of the Grand-Morin, *The Marne at the Joinville Bridge* (1927), *The Church at Chaville, The Pond at Ville d'Avray,*** Versailles, *The Sluice Gate at Moret* (about 1935–1937). We should mention that it is difficult to draw up an accurate chronology of Segonzac's works; the repetitiveness of the permanent themes and the carelessness of the artist himself in this regard have meant that there are only a few of his works whose dates we can confirm with certainty. However, accuracy about this would be for the most part fairly unimportant, considering the extent to which the work of Dunoyer de Segonzac presents an integrated and indivisible whole. It is even possible that the painter himself wanted to encourage this uncertainty that pointed up the continuity of his aesthetic progress. The surest landmarks are provided by the engravings and the publication dates of the engraved works and the illustrated books; a comparison of the themes treated both in engravings and in paintings enables us to perceive the correlation between these works. Still lifes, whose composition was now carefully planned, sometimes majestic, sometimes (as is frequently the case with the watercolors) extraordinarily lively and exploding with color, punctuated this period. Segonzac grouped together on a table or stand, either in an interior or in the sun on the terrace of « Le Maquis, » a parasol, a Panama hat, a basket, a newspaper, the soup tureen of Moustiers, flowers, and fruits. The accessories never varied. The very simple compositions appear to flow most naturally from the initial orderly grouping of objects, which the hand of the artist placed on the table that serves to support them. Yet there does exist a difference in nuance between one and the other. A particular watercolor, of a very wide format, is a simple sheaf of flowers and could well be the symbol of the summertime it evokes; another painting, whose composition specifically stresses vertical lines, is more contrived.

All these years were also marked by the concentrated production of different book illustrations and series of Segonzac engravings. 1929 was devoted to the engraving of plates intended to serve as illustrations for the novel by Charles-Louis Philippe, « Bubu of Montparnasse, » a project undertaken at the instigation of his friend, Régis Gignoux.*** This proved to be one of the artist's most brilliant successes. The novel had first been published in 1901. Editions illustrated by Granjouan (1905) and Charles Laborde (1924) were actually published; projected editions illustrated by Marquet and Steinlen were never completed. It was definitely left up to Segonzac, long after the death of the author and after the period when the novel took place, to bring to life once again the story of the young prostitute, Berthe, of Pierre, and of Bubu. Since the Left Bank had changed radically, he tried to find the models for the characters in the shady hotels of the Boulevard Sébastopol and the Rue Saint-Denis, in hospital wards and at local public dances. The studies devoted to Segonzac's illustration of the novel by Charles-Louis Philippe recall the genesis of the work. Thanks to Dr. Henri Mondor and to Dr. Pasteur Vallery-Radot, his friends, Dunoyer de Segonzac had the opportunity to sit in on the consultations in the Beaujon Hospital and to go along on the morning rounds of the Saint-Louis Hospital. He also went into the rooms of bug-ridden hotels to engrave at the scene or, failing that, to do pen sketches of the stupefied and somewhat anxious « girls, » amazed by the request of their « client. » These incidents point up what the artist felt was his need to live the scenes he described. Slightly more than a third of the plates thus engraved from life were retained and used to illustrate the book. This last fact shows how exacting Segonzac was when it came to his own work, a trait that was a necessary counterbalance to his apparent facility. The etchings in « Bubu » took advantage of most of the

---

* See p. 61.   ** See p. 73.   *** See p. 50.

GUYANCOURT, c. 1950–1955. Pen and watercolor on paper, $21^3/_4'' \times 29^{15}/_{16}''$ (55 × 76 cm)
Private collection, Paris

technical resources that helped form the style of the engraver: the delicate, rapid strokes were offset by the tiny, meticulous markings of the background; the needle drew wavering lines and nervous zigzag strokes that were abruptly broken off; areas carefully worked contrasted strongly with pure white surfaces. For the first time since Segonzac had undertaken to illustrate a literary work, here was a book of large format in a deluxe edition. Its immediate success did a great deal to enhance the celebrity of the artist.

A more modest project was the illustration of «Call of the Clown,» a comedy in one act by Régis Gignoux, who had enthusiastically encouraged Segonzac's efforts with «Bubu.» Régis Gignoux, a friend of Dorgelès, was the drama critic of «Le Figaro.» His text, which recounted the story of a clown, was only a pretext for the cooperation of Segonzac, who had always adored the theatre. Here again, he executed his engravings directly from life, as well as some drawings done sometimes at the Cirque d'Hiver, where the Fratellinis were performing, sometimes at the Théâtre de l'Empire in the loge of the famous Grocq, and finally in the Casino de Paris, where he portrayed Thérèse Dorny in her box, one of his best-known plates.

As a matter of fact, it was thanks to Thérèse Dorny, who later became his wife, that Segonzac made the acquaintance of Colette, in Saint-Tropez, prior to 1927. The writer wanted Segonzac, (whose art in many of its aspects was a reflection of her own artistic ideal,) to illustrate «Birth of the Day,» in which she evoked, as it happened, an artist whom she called the «Grand Dédé.» This project never came to fruition because it was eventually a friend of Segonzac's, Luc-Albert Moreau, who completed the assignment. Therefore, Colette wrote «The Grape Trellis,» named after her house in Saint-Tropez. Engraving alongside her as she wrote, Segonzac evoked the house, the cats, the bitch dog Soucy, the trellis, the table beneath the arbor and, above all, Colette, either seated at her little desk or in profile, all disheveled.* The work appeared in 1932, published by the artist himself, and although it was undoubtedly the most immediately appealing of any volume Segonzac had illustrated, it sold poorly at the time it was published. Subsequently, however, it became a work most sought after by bibliophiles. Colette, who was very fond of the book, wrote: «[Segonzac] on this occasion has created an admirable collection of the light and airy drawings into which he puts so much skill and artfulness. He has drawn ... my very modest house, thereby doing it a great honor and enshrining it, in a manner of speaking, in a Hall of Fame.» (Jean Adhémar in the catalogue of the exhibition at the Bibliothèque Nationale in 1958). Rarely has such intimacy, such shared inspiration and reciprocal respect been seen between author and illustrator. The portrait of Colette, that at first sight somewhat surprised the model, is one of the most lifelike any artist was ever inspired to execute. Segonzac was not basically a portraitist. We do not know of any painted self-portraits by the artist — something unusual — except for a few portraits in ink, highlighted with wash. It was through drawings, and more especially engravings, that he depicted for posterity the features of Jules Romains (1921), Dr. Henri Mondor (1944), André Gide (1946), Léon-Paul Fargue (1949), and Paul Léautaud (1950). Three portraits of Colette are also to be found among the etchings published in 1936, which illustrated the «Fourth Notebook of Colette» and were issued by Daragnès, who had printed «Bubu.»

In 1926 Segonzac had exhibited at the Galerie Marseille, then in 1928 at Georges Bernheim. After 1928, he exhibited more frequently in foreign countries than in Paris. Between 1929, the date of his first trip to the United States, and 1940, the works of Segonzac were frequently shown in America; an important milestone was his winning of the Carnegie award in 1933. In 1934 he was honored by being given the grand prize of the Biennale in Venice.

---

* See p. 59.

In 1935 an altogether exceptional book was published, «Cuisine, a Collection of 117 Recipes,» edited by Henry-Jean Laroche. The latter, a businessman as well as a sophisticated collector who had assembled, in his apartment near the Parc Monceau, a very fine selection of Impressionist works that he donated to the Musées Nationaux, was also a gourmet. He often invited artists to sumptuous gastronomic repasts. Dunoyer de Segonzac, Villebœuf, and Vuillard, all of whom were guests at one of these dinners, decided, in order to honor their host, to illustrate, each according to his own preference, a collection of recipes compiled by Laroche. Vuillard created six lithographs evoking the house and its owner, and Villebœuf did six etchings that were a humorous treatment of culinary history. Segonzac did six etchings (*Fish, Boiled Beef, Pig's Head, Fowl and Game, Mutton, Calf's Head*), which were supposed to represent the «contents of a kitchen.» Supplementing these plates prepared for «Cuisine,» Segonzac did some others on the same subject, several of which were subsequently issued separately. This unexpected introduction of one of the artist's favorite subjects, still lifes, into his engravings is not the least interesting aspect of this work, initially conceived as an amusing improvisation, which was the pretext for one of the most fascinating series by the artist.

In 1937, a large exhibition of his engravings, accompanied by drawings and watercolors, was organized at the Bibliothèque Nationale. The emphasis thus placed on his graphic works undoubtedly accounted in part for the subsidiary position given his efforts as a painter. It is true that, beginning in this period, the artist focused his attention on the etchings projected as illustrations for Virgil's «Georgics.» The first thought of this project is generally assumed to have been in 1920. At that time, Roger Allard and Segonzac drew up a list of ideal works calling for illustration for the prestigious «Nouvelle Revue Française.» First of all, the «Georgics» by Virgil, as well as a selection of «Sonnets» by the XVIth century French poet Ronsard, which he did illustrate for a new 1956 edition. From the moment he settled in Saint-Tropez, the memories of classical antiquity appear to have inspired figures bathed in sunlight called *Antiope, Ceres*, and *Bacchus*. It was after the publication of «The Grape Trellis» by Colette in 1932 that Vollard asked Segonzac to illustrate another collection by Colette; the artist preferred Virgil, and the choice fell on the «Georgics,» in the translation by Michel de Marolles. «It was Vollard who decided on the format, but it was I who imagined the country settings. . . . I executed more than three hundred etchings for the "Georgics"; none were engraved in the studio, and all expressed the eternal themes of rural life. . . . It was Virgil's feeling for the world of flowers and trees that I tried to re-create graphically. This was a source of inspiration for the great Latin poet; it was a form of pantheism that I have tried to communicate and identify with.» (A. Lioré, P. Cailler, «Engravings» Vol. V, 1965, pp. 11–14). Only one hundred and nineteen etchings were retained, Segonzac having put aside a large number of plates engraved between 1927 and 1930 because of their format, which he considered either too small or too large. The text was printed in Garamond type (invented, as we know, on the order of François I) on the presses of the Imprimerie Nationale. The first canto, having to do with work in the wheat fields, evoked almost exclusively the Ile-de-France: *Wheat Fields near Rennemoulin, Orchards of Chavenay, Oat Field near Villepreux, Haystacks near Saint-Cyr-sous-Dourdan*, and *Hills near Rochefort-en-Yvelines* were the scenes chosen to illustrate the Latin poet. The second canto, devoted to wine and work in the vineyards, quite naturally evoked Provence, Saint-Tropez, and its environs, Cogolin, Sainte-Anne Hill, and the road of the Môle. The third canto, which described the care of cattle, was engraved in Provence and the Ile-de-France. Finally, the fourth canto, devoted to bees, was illustrated almost entirely with scenes of Provence, although certain plates were direct evocations of the beehives of Chaville. The first plates were shown at the 1937 exhibition of the Bibliothèque Nationale; however, the death of

Castle of Grimaud, 1954
Pen and wash on charcoal sketch on paper, 21¹/₄" × 29⁵/₁₆" (54 × 74.5 cm)
Musée National d'Art Moderne. Centre National d'Art et de Culture Georges Pompidou, Paris

Vollard and the war delayed the publication of the two volumes of the «Georgics,» which were finally published by Segonzac himself in 1947 and shown for the first time as a complete unit in 1948 at the Galerie Charpentier. Nevertheless, at no time did the cohesiveness of the work appear to suffer because of this long gestation. On the contrary, the illustrations for the «Georgics» * proved to be a summing up of the universe in which Segonzac moved. The technical perfection and the nobility of the tone, which carried the cachet of the original, but was imbued throughout with an unfailing lyricism, make this work Segonzac's masterpiece. It must be included in a list of the most beautifully illustrated books of this century.

THE LAST YEARS (1950–1974)

The publication of the «Georgics» in 1948 coincided with the first great retrospective show of the artist's work. That same year, the Kunstalle in Basel also organized an exhibition. Another important exhibition took place in Switzerland in 1951, the very year when the major work by Claude Roger-Marx devoted to the artist was published.

Until his death in 1974, there was a succession of tributes paid to the artist: in 1955, at the Musée de Nice; in 1958, at the Bibliothèque Nationale; in 1959, in London, at the Royal Academy; in 1969, in Paris, at the Galerie Charpentier; and in 1972, at the Galerie Durand-Ruel. Exhibitions of his engravings were arranged in the Bibliothèque de Versailles, in Blois, Vichy, and Mulhouse. Between 1958 and 1970 the eight volumes of the catalogue raisonné of the artist's engravings were issued in Geneva, thanks to Pierre Cailler and Antoinette Lioré. In 1964 the artist received the official medal of the city of Paris. In 1969, his native town, Boussy-Saint-Antoine, honored him by naming a public square after him, and the house where he was born became the town's city hall.

In 1963 Dunoyer de Segonzac donated to the Musée National d'Art Moderne in Paris a significant group of his works (including *The Drinkers*, *The Picnic*, *The Couple*, etc., plus some watercolors and drawings), which supplemented the acquisitions previously made by the state and which recently has been augmented, thanks to a donation in payment of the death duties of the artist. Other donations were received by the Musée Lambinet and the Bibliothèque de Versailles, by the Musée de l'Ile-de-France, and the Musée des Deux Guerres; the generosity of these gifts can be measured by taking account of the exhibitions organized to show them. The Bibliothèque Nationale possesses a particularly rich store of prints and books illustrated by the artist.

Up to the very end of his life, Segonzac retained the sureness of hand and eye that is such an essential ingredient of his finest drawings and watercolors. A whole series of works, still revolving around the motif of Provence and Saint-Tropez, carry dates from 1950 to 1970. There are landscapes of Bormes, of Grimaud, of the Gulf of Saint-Tropez and the mountains of the Maures, of the Estérel, of the Bay of the Cannebiers, of Collobrières, of the valley of the Môle, and more. The Ile-de-France remained a region he preferred, and each of its villages, towns, and cities inspired a work: Provins, Crécy-en-Brie, Couilly, Périgny, Chennevières, Senlisse, Guyancourt, Villepreux, Chaville, Ville d'Avray, Versailles, Saint-Cloud, Bougival, Marly, Triel, Feucherolles, Poissy, Auxerre, and even Paris itself. Notre-Dame, and the bridges and the quays of the Seine gave the artist a reason to create luminous watercolors with vividly realized details.

---

* See pp. 72 and 75.

True, still lifes remained a major concern, and it was a still life of flowers that the artist left on his easel when he died.

After the «Georgics,» Segonzac continued his activity as a book illustrator. One of the first works that appeared, in 1949, was entitled «Burning Coasts,» 1928–1938, and illustrated a text by Léon-Paul Fargue. In addition to two original etchings (one being a portrait of L. P. Fargue), this volume reproduced a series of watercolor «notes» made on the beaches of Provence in the period between the two world wars. It was Léon-Paul Fargue himself, in Paris and immobilized by illness, who asked Segonzac, whom he greatly admired, to illustrate one of his books. In response, Segonzac proposed using some watercolors depicting the beaches of the Côte d'Azur and Saint-Tropez, where Fargue himself had lived. He specified, in the foreword that preceded the text that described the poet's recollections: «Burning Coasts» [this can also mean «Burning Ribs»], Thérèse Dorny exclaimed one day as she watched nudes broiling in the sun on the burning sand. This expression was employed as the title of the book. There was another work that also paid homage to a friend; it was «Pierre Falké, Our Friend,» and was published in 1950. Segonzac had known Pierre Falké (1887–1947) at the front, during the 1914–1918 war. The latter was an illustrator and a member of the circle of humorists of Montmartre; it was Montmartre that furnished Segonzac with the principal subjects treated in the nine etchings done for the book.

Even more important was the artist's contribution in the form of illustrations for the novel «The Ivy,» by Pierre Brisson, director of «Le Figaro,» which was published in 1953. The novel, written at the time the author had taken refuge near Lyons during the Second World War, evoked his recollections of Paris, Versailles, Marseilles, and Lyons. At the request of Pierre Brisson, whom he had known for a long time, Segonzac was very tempted to turn his hand once again to some of his favorite subjects. The twenty-eight etchings conceived for this volume are notable for their depiction of barges on the Seine, at Bougival and Andrésy, the Pont-des-Arts, the Moulin Rouge and Montmartre, the church of Guyancourt, which is also the subject of a superb watercolor, and the park of the château at Versailles. In 1955, shortly after «The Ivy,» there appeared the «Sonnets» by Ronsard, on which, according to Segonzac's own statement, he had worked from 1948 to 1956. For the text, he selected the same Garamond type he had employed for the Latin text of the «Georgics.» Faithful to his concept of what an illustrator should be, he attempted to retrace the steps taken by the poet and to revisit the places frequented by Ronsard: Vendôme, Pont-de-Braye, Bourgueil, the banks of the Loire. Marie, Cassandra, and Helen were brought back to life, elegant figures without any affectations. «I sought,» Segonzac declared, «to evoke graphically the spirit of the poet, his extreme sensitivity, his discreet and tender sensuality, and his love for the earth of his native land.» (A Lioré, P. Cailler, «Engravings,» Vol. VII, 1968).

We should also mention one last work that, in addition to drawings by Segonzac engraved on wood by Jacques Beltrand, contained fifteen etchings by the artist; we refer to a book with text by Jean Giraudoux, «Sport.» Between 1926 and 1936, Dunoyer de Segonzac had executed a whole series of pen drawings and etchings intended to illustrate a volume by Jean Giraudoux on sports, but the project had not come to immediate fruition. It was only after the death of Giraudoux that Segonzac decided to make use of some old etchings and supplemented them with a new series to make up the illustrations for the book, which was issued in 1963. This incident illustrates well the artist's fidelity to the subjects he preferred and continued to treat throughout his career.

Prolific until the very end of his life, the artist was blessed by a happy conclusion to his long activity. Segonzac knew fame, but never made a conscious effort to achieve it. His modesty, his love for his profession, and the loyalty of his friendships are always recalled by those who knew him. His long life gave him the opportunity to witness all of the major events that made their mark

STILL LIFE (PEDESTAL TABLE AND GARDEN SHEARS), undated
Watercolor, 22″ × 30½″ (56 × 77,5 cm). Collection: Mrs Sam Salz, New York

STILL LIFE (FLOWER VASE AND LEMONS), 1974
Pen and watercolor on paper, 22¹/₆″ × 29¹⁵/₁₆″ (56 × 76 cm). Private collection, Paris

on the history of art in the twentieth century, but, with the exception of his penchant for Cubism, he does not appear to have been particularly affected by any of them.

Claude Roger-Marx, in the last preface that he wrote for Segonzac, on the occasion of the exhibition at the Orangerie in the Tuileries in 1976, did not hesitate to declare him to be the «opposite» of Picasso, who had died only one year before Segonzac. This brief comment, coming from a critic who had known him and who had defended him better than any other single individual, defines the artist's attitude very accurately. The profound significance of Segonzac's art is brilliantly summarized in this profession of faith: «I have always thought that an artist should have absolute freedom to express himself, that his work should be completely personal, not be subject to any external rules, whether dogmas of the past or of the present, and express the beauty of life, of light, of nature as he feels it, freely and independently. It is time alone that will evaluate his work. It will endure if it is authentic; if it is artificial, it will be ephemeral. I have always been of the opinion that art, in order to last, should be simple and truthful.»

Ramatuelle, undated. Ink drawing and wash, 15¾" × 22¾" (40 × 58 cm)
Collection: Mrs Sam Salz, New York

BIOGRAPHY

1884–1900 Born in Boussy-Saint-Antoine (Val-de-Marne) on July 7, 1884. Childhood spent in Paris and Boussy. Studied at Louis-le-Grand and Henri IV schools. Graduated in 1900.

1900–1907 Frequented different private studios (studios of Luc-Olivier Merson, Jean-Paul Laurens, and the Académie de la Palette, whose staff included Prinet, Desvallières, Jacques-Emile Blanche, and Charles Guérin). Made friends with some other young artists, Mainssieux, Luc-Albert Moreau, and Boussingault, with whom he rented a studio at 37 rue Saint-André-des-Arts, Paris.

1908 First stay in Saint-Tropez. First submission to the Salon d'Automne.

1909 First submission to the Salon des Indépendants.

1910 Exhibited at the Indépendants and the Salon d'Automne *A Cabaret*, also called *The Drinkers,* that was acquired by the famous couturier Paul Poiret. At Poiret's, Dunoyer de Segonzac was to meet Max Jacob, Dufy, and Vlaminck. Publication of the album devoted to Isadora Duncan and also the « Scheherazade » album.

1911 Exhibited at the Indépendants, in Paris and in Brussels, at the Salon d'Automne and at one group show. Second exhibition of the Norman Society of Modern Painting, at the Galerie d'Art Contemporain, 4 rue Tronchet.

1912 Exhibited at the Indépendants, also the Salon d'Automne, as well as group shows with the Cubists (Paris, offices of the periodical « La Vie, » 68 rue Mazarine, the « Salon de la Section d'Or, » Galerie La Boétie, and the Galerie Druet; and in Berlin, « III Jury freie Kunstschau, » Kunsthaus Lepke). Left the studio of the Rue Saint-André-des-Arts to take another, at 13 rue Bonaparte, where Derain also lived.

1913 A cruise on the Mediterranean with Poiret (Corsica, Naples, Sicily, Tunisia, Granada, Algeria). Exhibited at the Indépendants, the Salon d'Automne, the Armory Show in New York, Chicago, and Boston, as well as in several group shows in Paris (Galerie Marseille), in Amsterdam (Stedelijk Museum), and in London (Doré Galleries). Illustrated « Bittersweet Songs » by his friend, Francis Carco.

1914 First one-man show in Paris, at the Galerie Levesque (later the Galerie Barbazanges), 109 rue du Faubourg Saint-Honoré (preface of catalogue by René-Jean; exhibited at the Indépendants.
Drafted in August and left Saint-Tropez to join his corps in Fontainebleau.

1914–1918 War drawings published in « L'Elan » and « Le Crapouillot. » Finished the war as a second lieutenant in charge of camouflage of the third army and was awarded the Croix de Guerre. His war drawings were exhibited at the Galerie Marseille in 1917 and 1918.

1919 Exhibited with Luc-Albert Moreau in Paris at the Galerie Devambez, 43 boulevard Malesherbes, and at the Salon d'Automne. Illustrated « The Wooden Crosses » by Roland Dorgelès, a volume published in 1921. For this work the artist took up etching, the rudiments of which he was taught by J. E. Laboureur.

1920 Exhibited in Paris, in the Galeries Druet, Crès, Marseille, at the Indépendants and at the Salon d'Automne, also in London's Independent Gallery. From this period on, Segonzac frequently stayed in Chaville.

1921 Exhibited at the Indépendants and the Salon d'Automne.
Worked during the winter in Saint-Nom-la-Bretèche.

1922–1923 Participated in the Salon d'Automne in 1922; illustrated « Picture of Boxing, » by his friend Tristan Bernard.
Exhibited at the Independent Gallery.

1924 Spent a working vacation in Serbonne in the Valley of Morin.
Exhibited in Paris at the Galerie Barbazanges and in London at Colnaghi's.

1925 Together with Luc-Albert Moreau and Villebœuf, purchased from Camoin the property « Le Maquis » in Saint-Tropez, where his stays became more and more frequent and longer and longer.
The works of Segonzac caused a sensation at the Paul Poiret auction, November 18, 1925.

1926 Exhibited at the Galerie Marseille in Paris. Acquisition by the Musée du Luxembourg of *Farm at Aire.*

1927 Exhibited in London at the Independent Gallery.
Worked in Joinville-le-Pont and in the Valley of the Marne.

1928 Exhibited in Paris at the Galerie Georges Bernheim (successor to Galerie Barbazanges).

1929 First trip to the United States in the autumn. Publication of « Bubu of Montparnasse » by Charles-Louis Philippe, illustrated with etchings by Segonzac.

1931 Stayed in Moret-sur-Loing.

1932 Publication of « The Grape Trellis » by Colette, illustrated with etchings by Segonzac.

1933 Given the Carnegie award.
Grand prize for painting at Venice Biennale.

1935 Illustrated « Cuisine » by Henry-Jean Laroche with Vuillard and Villebœuf.

1937 Exhibition of « Engravings, Drawings, and Watercolors » of the artist at the Bibliothèque Nationale (preface by Claude Roger-Marx). Exhibited at the Salon d'Automne.

1938 Exhibited at the Salon des Indépendants and in Chicago.

1939 Exhibited in the Musée des Arts Décoratifs, Paris.

1947 Elected a member of the Royal Academy, London.

1948 Retrospective exhibition and display of the « Georgics, » illustrated by the artist, who had been working on it since 1928, at the Galerie Charpentier, Paris (preface by Claude Roger-Marx).
Retrospective exhibition in Kunsthalle, Basel (preface by J. Laran).

1951 Retrospective exhibition at the Musée d'Art et d'Histoire, Geneva (preface by Claude Roger-Marx).

1953 Illustrated « The Ivy » by Pierre Brisson.

1955 Retrospective exhibition at the Musée de Nice (engravings and watercolors); preface by Claude Roger-Marx.
Publication of « Sonnets » by Pierre de Ronsard, illustrated by Segonzac.

1957 Exhibited at the Salon d'Automne.

1958 Exhibition at the Bibliothèque Nationale (engravings); preface by J. Cain, essay by J. Vallery-Radot, catalogue by J. Adhémar.

1959 Exhibition at Royal Academy, London (introduction by J. Vallery-Radot).

1960 Retrospective exhibition at the Galerie Charpentier, Paris (preface by R. Nacenta and Claude Roger-Marx).

1963 Gift to the Musée National d'Art Moderne in Paris (B. Dorival, « Revue du Louvre, » 1963, no. 6, pp. 289–94), to the Musée Lambinet and the Bibliothèque de Versailles.

1964 Grand Medal of the City of Paris; exhibition at the Bibliothèque de Versailles (engravings).

1965 Gift to the Musée de l'Ile-de-France at Sceaux (catalogue by G. Poisson, preface by J. Héron de Villefosse).
The artist married the actress, Thérèse Dorny.

1966 Exhibition in New York at the Acquavella Galleries (preface by Claude Roger-Marx).

1967 Exhibition in Oslo (engravings) and at the Château of Blois (engravings; catalogue by R. Passeron).
Gift to the Musée des Deux Guerres Mondiales (catalogue by the widow of General A. M. Barthe).

1968 Exhibited at the Salon des Indépendants (1906–1909 retrospective).

1969 Exhibited at the Salon des Indépendants (1910 retrospective).
Inauguration of a square named after the artist in the town of his birth, Boussy-Saint-Antoine. (The house where he was born, which became the town hall, houses a small museum.)

1971 Exhibition in the Centre Culturel Valéry Larbaud at Vichy (book illustrations; preface by Dr. J. Lacarin, introduction by J. Guignard, catalogue by M. Kuntz).

1972 Retrospective exhibition at the Galerie Durand-Ruel, Paris (preface by Claude Roger-Marx).

1973 Exhibition at the Bibliothèque de Mulhouse (engravings).

1974 The artist died in Paris on September 17, 1974; he is buried in Saint-Tropez.

Posthumous exhibitions and tributes

1975 Musée de l'Athénée, Geneva (preface by J. M. Kyriazi).

1976 Paris, Orangerie in the Tuileries (preface by Claude Roger-Marx, introduction by Hélène Adhémar, who had discussed plans for this exhibition with the artist, catalogue by Anne Distel).

1978 Paris, Grand-Palais, Watercolor Section.

1979 Tokyo.

BIBLIOGRAPHY

We shall only list the works entirely devoted to Dunoyer de Segonzac. The bibliographies in these monographs refer to articles in newspapers and periodicals that are not mentioned here, although some of those articles are quoted in the text. One should also see the catalogues of exhibitions.

RENÉ-JEAN. *A. Dunoyer de Segonzac.* Paris: N.R.F. (collection Les Peintres Français Nouveaux, no. 11), 1922.

ROGER-MARX, Claude. *Dunoyer de Segonzac.* Paris: Crès, 1925.

GUENNE, Jacques. *Dunoyer de Segonzac.* Paris: Marcel Seheur, 1928.

JAMOT, Paul. *Dunoyer de Segonzac.* Paris: Floury, 1929 (revised edition, Paris, 1941).

GAUTHIER, Maximilien. *A. Dunoyer de Segonzac.* Paris: Les Gémeaux, 1949.

ROGER-MARX, Claude. *Dunoyer de Segonzac.* Geneva: Pierre Cailler, 1951.

DORIVAL, Bernard, and HAUERT, Roger. *Dunoyer de Segonzac.* Geneva: René Kister, 1956.

LIORÉ, Antoinette, and CAILLER, Pierre. *Catalogue de l'Œuvre Gravé de Dunoyer de Segonzac*, a catalogue raisonné of his etchings. Geneva: Pierre Cailler, 1958–1970, 8 volumes.

FOUCHET, Max-Paul. *A. Dunoyer de Segonzac, Saint-Tropez et la Provence.* Paris: Morancé, 1964.

FOSCA, François. *Segonzac-Provence.* Lausanne-Paris: Bibliothèque des Arts, 1969

PASSERON, Roger. *Les Gravures de Dunoyer de Segonzac.* Paris: Bibliothèque des Arts, 1970.

André Dunoyer de Segonzac-Dessins 1900–1970. Geneva: Pierre Cailler, 1970.

HUGAULT, Henri. *Dunoyer de Segonzac.* Paris: Bibliothèque des Arts, 1973.

Dunoyer de Segonzac-Watercolors, with a hitherto unpublished text by the artist and a study of his work as a watercolorist by Roger PASSERON. Neuchatel: Ides et Calendes, 1976.

KYRIAZI, Jean Melas. *André Dunoyer de Segonzac, sa vie, son œuvre.* Lausanne: Harmonies et Couleurs, 1976.

We wish to thank the owners of the pictures reproduced herein, as well as those collectors who did not wish to have their names mentioned:

MUSEUMS

Bibliothèque Nationale, Paris – Musée d'Art Moderne de la Ville de Paris – Musée des Deux Guerres Mondiales, Paris – Musée National d'Art Moderne. Centre National d'Art et de Culture Georges Pompidou, Paris – Musée du Louvre. Cabinet des Dessins, Paris – Musée de l'Annonciade, Saint-Tropez – Musée Lambinet, Versailles – Musées Nationaux – Museum of Modern Art, Teheran – The Tate Gallery, London – The Metropolitan Museum of Art, New York.

PRIVATE COLLECTIONS

Mr and Mrs David Evins, New York – Jerome K. Ohrbach, Beverly Hills, California – Mrs Sam Salz, New York – Mrs Jane Robinson Sidney, Beverly Hills, California – Dr and Mrs Howard D. Sirak, Columbus, Ohio.

LIST OF ILLUSTRATION